Walking the Shadow

Martin Karlík

BookLeaf Publishing

India | USA | UK

Presentation by *BookLeaf Publishing*

Web: www.bookleafpub.com

E-mail: info@bookleafpub.com

ISBN:9789360943110

First edition 2024

ACKNOWLEDGEMENT

I am grateful to my mom, my dad and my sisters for always being there for me. I am grateful to my closest friends on Ørestads Boulevard for being the best friends I could wish for -- even when I make a peanut butter strawberry soup, or when I boil sesame seeds instead of couscous. I am grateful to my friends from back home, and to all my friends that I made in Aalborg, in Copenhagen and in Mumbai. Lastly, I am grateful to all the lovely strangers that I stumbled upon during my travels. Every single person that I ever met has been a teacher to me.

DEDICATION

I dedicate this poetry collection to the monks and the little girls from Khawalung Tashi Choeling Monastery in Kathmandu.

PREFACE

Hi.

I didn't mean to interrupt, but
I got something on my mind, and
I guess I thought that...
If I just tried...
Well, whatever. Hope you like.

If You're Sad, Please Reconsider

Please read slow.
We don't have time
To be rushing places now.

And I don't have much to share,
Just a thought to leave behind:

If you're sad,
Please reconsider.
If it's really worth your while.

If you're sad

Please reconsider

I like you better when you smile.

Where I'm From

I am from
      a different voice
From Lego bricks
      and manuals
I am from
      the curious, brave, yet self-abusive
designers of riots.

I am from
      a script I wrote
A vision
      I can barely hold
A butterfly
      I never caught
But the most of me
      is void
And, at last —
      the quiet.

19:57

Not spoken to, but spoken at —
What you get used to…
Nods that don't mean nothing more
Than "Let me go".

Was it right? To listen
Without caring no more.
Was it wrong? For my advice
Be "I don't know".

The sunrise room went empty
As I couldn't stay there…
The quiet voice got louder
And it found its tone.

The clock
Got stuck
At three minutes to time-to-be-gone

And I never
Corrected it
Evermore.

Mountains

There used to be mountains, you know?
Unfolding over the fields.
I would just stare at them slow,
Imagine what I could be.

There was no way I could count
The trees that covered their peaks,
I would just stand there and smile,
And let them stare back at me.

And when the winter months came,
And the stars seasoned the sky,
I let the freezing, dry air
Stare at them with me awhile.

But as the trees tend to grow,
As mountains tend to get climbed,
I had to walk away slow,
I had to leave them behind.

There used to be mountains, you know?
Now there's a fjord and two seas.
But I'd like to believe, you know?!
That there are still mountains in me.

I Was Looking

5

I was looking at the world
From this viewpoint of my own.
Was it perfect? Not quite, no.
But good enough.

I was looking at my past,
Those unresolved storylines.
Should I scratch them off my mind,
Or solve at last?

I was looking at you, dear.
Oh, how strange you made me feel.
Was that kiss you gave me real?
Or just a fable of my mind?

I was looking, I was there.
I was one heart's beat away.
You looked at me, as if to say:
"Just get out!"

I was looking all around
For some truthful peace of mind,
Which would leave me satisfied
With whom I'm not.

But all that I could see out there —
In the fjord, its shades of grey,
In its lonesome, confused waves,
Was who I am.

I was looking at the world
Through this see-through terrace door.
Was it perfect? I don't know.
You tell me that.

Let's Row Homeward

We left our problems — yours and mine —
Hanging on a cotton line
Like laundry, drying on the sun
To be picked up once this is done
And rowed into the starry night.
Just a kayak, beers and smokes.

The waves would argue with our try
To match the melody and rhyme
Of the moments flowing by…
If you tried to grab just one,
We'd lose the rhythm, and your harm
Would bring the kayak to a stop…
So don't.

We kept on rowing. When the stars
Flash upon the Nordic sky,
You don't need a reason why,
You just row, no questions asked,
Into the calm. This sleepy town
Would not wake up, no not tonight…
Yeah, not tonight.

As we got stranded in the dark,
We let our visions — yours and mine —

Flow upward the starry sky.
And if you stalked us from aside,
Grabbed a flashlight. Raised it high.
And pointed it toward my eyes,
You just might have seen me smile…

…

- "Let's row homeward."
- "Think it's time?"
- "Think it's time."

I Made My Move

I made my move. And out of all
The stories that I could have told
I chose this one. I chose to go
Where the stars await my soul.

I made my move. It wasn't hard…
Sure, took time to figure out.
Was is the best one? Maybe not.
But the best that I could find.
That's gotta mean something, right?
… Right?

I made my move. I took a chance,
I looked the mirror in the face,
And I saw it cannot be that bad
To go and live your very best.

I made my move. I turned and stared
At this crossroad over there:
The dust, which used to lead the way,
Now whirled and floated through the air
As if to tell me: "Don't look there,
The past is past: the good, the bad
Will always stay right here, my friend,
But you chose to walk away,

That choice is now yours to bear
So go and walk the path you have
Designed so well!"

So… I made my move. It's quiet now.
All the dust has settled down.
No more doubts to waste my while,
No more thoughts to tell me how
To play the game. This time around

I made my move. It's time to go.
Was it right or was it wrong?
Don't look back, don't ruin the show!
It doesn't matter anymore…
I made my move, it's settled now.
Don't you question where and why!
I made my move...

It's your turn now.

Knock on the Door

Someone called, I turned around —
Perhaps the wind…
Someone knocked... It was my heart
From within.

I kept still. I let it leave —
Cause I did not
Want it see — the mess in me —
The ignored dust.

I let it leave. It did not go,
It knocked again.
I rose to feet, I tried real hard
To understand

What it wants, and why am I
The one it seeks.
I got my plans, and work to be —
Be busy with.

I got my life. Now go away!
Don't want you here…
You'd tell me things, that I don't think
I want to hear.

I heard a whisper: 'As you wish…'
Right from the door
And then the steps — the fading sound
Of cobblestone.

I rushed outside, I yelled out: 'Wait!'
What have I done…
But it was gone, wouldn't come back —
I saw that now.

And just like that, my only chance
For happiness…
Forever lost, in moment's worth
Of hesitance.

And then the wind, with all its force —
Believe or not —
Shut the door, and as such,
Has locked me out.

So here I stand, in pitch black air —
Nowhere to go.
It's not quite right, but neither wrong…
Just freezing cold.

It was a trap — whoever knocked
Just disappeared.
Without a trace… Took off and I'm
Left freezing here.

Such a random, somewhat shy
Knock on the door,
And now I'll walk — this pitch black path
Forevermore.

Puzzle Pieces

A sudden scream. An ancient roar
From the depths of my own core
In a somewhat frightened form:
"Do they know me? Do they know
Who I am, I mean — at all?"

Then, a face. An angry stare
From someone whose cross I bear,
As if I'm the one to blame
For this man's DIY hell.
We both smiled. The smile of bare,
Silent resignation — shared.
And muttered into empty air:
"I don't think I belong anywhere."

Bullet Points

In the absent-mindness of the thoughts,
In the tired waking of the soul,
I come to find displeasure in the way
We humans walk.

Such arrogant quality we have;
To think we can explain away the world.
To reason, in place of silent finding out
With humble stare at all that is unknown —
- Without the need to prove anything wrong
- Without expecting anything at all
- Without having to take a thought, and turn it
into
- A few bullet points.

What Is a Pond?

Is mind a pond?
Full of fish and fish-like creatures,
And are fish thoughts?

And if so,
Should you take care of it?
Clean it once in a while,
And look at it with curious critique when the sun
is setting —
Almost as if you cared for it?

And what happens?
When one fish outgrows the rest
And it dominates the pond —
And it cannot be defeated.

And maybe the fish is good.
Or maybe it is evil. Unimportant.
Should the pond keeper allow that?

And all the moonlit evening walks
By the pond,
With a fishing rod in your hand
When the fish aren't biting
And all you feel

Is a cold breeze coming from the woods
And it is lonely
And it is heart-breaking.

And there is nothing in the pond,
Not a fish that you would like to bite on,
Or even hold in your hands
And gently release back.

Pond
Can be a lovely place

Or
It can be a scary place

Is heart a pond?

I'll Build Myself an Island House

I'll build myself an island house.
I will live an island life.
I will write some island rhymes
And find my peace.

I will watch the sun grow tall,
In the summer, in the fall…
I will watch it come and go.
And set — repeat —

I will think back to my home,
To the dragons ever-tall,
The evening walks by moonlit fjord,
And then the sound of metro doors
Closing in.

I'll build myself an island house.
Right beneath the island stars
And all that birds will sing about
Will die with me.

I will sit down by the shore,
I will feel my smile unfold
And no one —

No one!
On this world
Will make me come back home.

Okay, I found my other sock... All good, never
mind.

At Nørreport Station

I grabbed a pole.
The metro train accelerates so rough.
I wonder if they could've made it smoother…
If the engineers thought of that or not
That people might be falling, when you
Wake them up, and
Make them continue their lives.

I'm anxious about wasting time by listening to
songs that I don't like.
And planning out my day:
And thus, worrying twice.

I notice a ticket-man, and my heartbeat shoots
up to the sky.
I have a ticket, but…
What if I have not?

I get off, and queue up for the escalator line.
There's people — so many that I can't…
The air is hard to breathe, and everything looks
industrial-grey.

The left side of the escalator is for people that
are rushing.

The right side is for people that are rushing, but
too tired to be rushing overtime.

I choose the left side, and walk by the standing
bodies —
Dragged along like stacks of clover my grandpa
used to carry on a trolley cart.
To feed the rabbits day and night…

I like to pretend that if I am walking, it is me
who chose the path.
Cause otherwise I'd be but a hamster in a wheel
that's running for his life.
And that — obviously! — I'm not.

Fuck
        this hamster-wheeling life.

I Am Becoming Resentful

Against my will
I'm finding myself slipping further.
Again and still
Take the girl, but please don't hurt her.

I made my way
From the bed into the shower.
It's still the same,
But with each day it's getting harder.

Can you tell
The thoughts of reason from the chatter?
I heard my name —
But I forgot how to bother.

Excuse me sir,
Could you, for my last sad dollar,
Tell her that…
That I said I couldn't find her?

Against my will,
Against the wind on roads to travel…
Again… Or still?
I am leaving. Take care, everybody.

Grand Canyon Thoughts

Westbound.
Remember! — Westbound.
All my trains — Westbound
Are running late.

But you see — Right now,
In orange and blue, how
Suddenly easy
Is to forget

The butterflies that I've been chasing
Amid the tall sunflower mazes
And the rhyme schemes I've been changing
Just like that ->

And now I am tired of chasing butterflies.

I will sit down on this grass
I will rest my weary thoughts
I will give my late Goodbye
To all that's drowned inside my mind
And I will watch these stars roll by.

I don't need no butterfly for now.

At the Arrivals

24

I came by —
I brought a book
To not look odd.
But I didn't
Read at all.
No… I just watched.

I watched people
Arrive from
Their other worlds.
I watched people
Making way
Back to their homes.

Way too many
Passed along
Without a hug.
And way too many
Didn't even
Hope for one.

And way too many
Didn't see
A waving flag
And way too many

Didn't get
To shake a hand.

Just passed along.

Right along.

Back to wherever it was that they believed that
they belong.

…

Funny place
To spend your time —
Arrivals gate.
I'd give it
Four out of five —
Can recommend.

The Calling's Claim

I heard a calling
And so I ran
Upon the beaches
With milky sand
Into the jungle —
The lion's den,
Over the mountains
And in my hand
Nothing but
A grasp of air
Which I could never
Take away
Only take in
And then exhale
As it was meant.

Just like a mother
Calls your name
For you to come
Not knowing where
Or how or why —
And in your hand
Nothing but
The calling's claim
That it's gonna

Be okay
If you just run.

And so I ran.

The Teacher of Love

From afar
I watched the teacher write the topic
Of today's class.

It read "Love".
And from the way the teacher spoke,
From the worn out piece of chalk,
From the scratches on the board
I could tell —
That this was not her first time teaching that.

It read "Love".
And from her look, so deep and wise,
From the passion in her eyes,
From the magic of her smile
I could tell —
That I better listen to what she's got to say.

It read "Love".
And everywhere the teacher walked,
She left roses on the floor,
For those brave enough to hope —
As if in Harry Potter's world
Some sort of "Anti-Dementor"
Was sucking sorrow out of those,

Those who needed it the most
And I could tell —
That there's no end to how much she can bear.

It read "Love".
But what it didn't read was how
The teacher knew so much about
This strange topic she called "Love"…
Where'd she learn it? How'd she find
The strength to believe through the night?
The patience and the will the fight?
And I could tell —
That nothing else than this subject has ever
really mattered anyway.

…

The class is over now.

As I'm walking my own path,
I'd like to say that I have passed,
Just to make the teacher proud,
But the truth is there's a lot
More to solve and figure out,
And I'd like to get this right.

And I need to get this right…

But for now, all that I got

From this class taught heart to heart:
Love is simple. Is it not?

All it takes is everything you've got.

Christmas in New Delhi

Selfish, I feel — To be alone.
To have chosen to come here by myself,
Keep all the love that should have been shared,
And fly away.

The skies outside are grey, not white,
The honks of Autos fill the night,
Ten million people walk the streets
But not from church — to make ends meet,
Last snow I saw was in a book
On dean's desk, named "Luxembourg",
Where pictures of their pretty land
Made me miss home once again,
Though mine is still far from theirs
But still… same same…

"Home" — such a beautiful word.
I think my favourite one of all…
The way its cozy meaning binds
With the fluffy way it sounds
And the power that it holds…
I cannot give it enough love
With just the words
And that's what hurts
The most.

But if you asked me where is home,
I'd shrug and smile, say "I don't know…"
But I'm not there — that is for sure.

Sunday at the Monastery

I went for chai
Outside our place.
Unsweetened —
Unlike my days.
It's been a while
Since I had stayed
In a place
Where I had played
A role of someone
Wanted there

So this felt new
And I had to
Take a break…

It was time
To return back
But I came late…

…

The little monk,
He asked me: "Sir,
Do you understand
This game we play?"

I said: "Sure,
I'll kick the ball
With you soon,
Little guy."

He said: "No.
No understand.
I don't think
You understand
This game we play.

In this game
You say you come,
But then you go
There outside.

We don't go
There outside…
We only play.

I don't think
You understand
This game we play."

Home Again

I'm home again.

It's been a while
Since I've seen these people smile,
Since I watched the sun go down
In this city I called "mine"
Once upon a distant time
It's been a while…

I'm home again.

Back in these streets…
Where the sky feels within reach,
And the air — so fresh to breath —
Gives me something to believe
Back in these streets.

I'm home again.

I see a road.
Waiting for me to be walked…
It seems so much longer though,
Than all the roads I've walked before.
Is it lonely? Is it cold?
Cause I am really sick of those…

And what stories does it hold?
I ask… No one answers though.
I don't think anyone knows.

Only the wind, that keeps the road
Safe from all of those who hope
That it will be smooth and short,
Whispers in-between its blows
In a fair, yet evil voice:

"You're home again.
I hope you know
What exactly is your home…"

I see a road.